Soapbox

Matt Krause

Delridge Press
Seattle MMXI

Copyright © 2011 Matt Krause
All rights reserved.
ISBN: 1463791275
ISBN-13: 978-1463791278

For Frank Kleist

Table of Contents

Andrei Kleist 1

The man at the fence 7

Learning to speak Big Kid 9

Twigs, rocks, dust 13

Truck stop 16

Drunk barber 18

Take a teacher to lunch 20

A parting gift from my grandpa 22

Muslims are the new niggers 30

Cold sweat 33

Go talk to your audience 34

I love running barefoot 36

Egg, cheese, toast 40

You don't get to blame society 41

My cousin's name is Jihad 44

More than just groceries 49

The first thing you should know 51

Looking, finding, ignoring 52

The ripples are why the cake tastes so good 52

You owe it to your country 54

Starbucks 55

Andrei Kleist

When I was about 15 years old, I was really into bicycle road racing. It was my life, my main activity. I spent almost every single hour of every single day either doing it, training for it, or learning how to train for it.

The thing was, I wasn't very good at it. In my small town in California I was one of the best at it. But when I'd go to a race where the other riders were coming from bigger ponds, I was well below average. In fact, I rarely even finished with the pack. I'd get dropped and then come straggling over the finish line long after the race had ended.

My best friend at the time was named Andrei Kleist, another rider from the same small town. Andrei and I were the same age, but we went to different high schools. That was okay, because neither of us thought much of school. We were both straight-A students, but there was too much bike racing to be done, and the world was too big a place to bother with high school.

Andrei had a natural talent on the bike I didn't. His talent was especially brilliant on the hills, the most difficult part of any course. When the rest of us were suffering up a hill, gasping for breath, thighs burning, working so hard we were almost blinded to the road in front of us, Andrei would float up from behind us, dancing on his pedals as if he didn't even realize what he was doing. He would glance over at us with this bored, nonchalant look, scream that spastic guttural scream of his that said, "I've had enough of this," and then he would magically, effortlessly accelerate and disappear around the bend ahead as if we had been standing still.

We would inevitably find him a half hour later at the top of the hill, sitting on a curb wondering why it had taken us so long. We all hated the fact he would never understand we had worked harder than he had, and yet we were the slow ones.

There's a story about Andrei, one I wasn't there that day to witness, but have no trouble believing...

When Andrei was 16 or 17, he was competing at a race in Northern California, a road race out in the rolling hills at the foot of the Sierras east of Sacramento. The older age groups were sharing the same course, and one of our grown-up friends, Bob Brooks (another very talented rider), came upon Andrei sitting on the side of the road, his bike leaned up against the dirt bank. Bob pulled over and asked Andrei why he had dropped out. Did he have a flat tire? Was there a big crash? Was he hurt?

Andrei shrugged his shoulders and said, "I don't know, I don't care, this is stupid." Bob was so dumbfounded he didn't know what to say, except, "Well then, get back on that bike and finish the race!"

Andrei hopped on his bike and started riding. He caught up with the pack, rested with them for a few miles, and then pulled ahead. Without even appreciating the magnitude of what he was doing, he dropped every single one of them and won the race so far ahead of the others the officials wondered if they had gotten lost.

Andrei was not racing against average schmucks that day. He was racing against the best of the best, young riders who would go on in a few years to race in the Olympics and the Tour de France.

By the time I was 17, Andrei and I had fallen out of touch. My family had moved out of state. In our new town my interest in cycling dwindled quickly, and by the time I went to college I barely even rode a bike often enough to remember I owned one.

Then one day when I was about 30 years old, my dad called to say he had some bad news. Andrei had been killed while riding in the foothills east of Fresno, California, where he lived at the time. He had run head first into an oncoming car while riding with his father on Tollhouse Road, one of his favorite courses. Descending around a blind corner, he had crossed the yellow line into oncoming traffic just in time to meet up with a Jeep coming the other way.

He was killed instantly, probably even before he landed on the pavement behind the Jeep. His dad, descending at a slower pace behind his son, came upon the scene a few minutes later.

I hadn't seen or heard from Andrei in over 12 years, but there was no question in my mind that I was going to the funeral. I hopped in my car and drove straight through overnight, arriving in town about 2 hours before the funeral.

After the funeral, I learned that as Andrei grew into adulthood, he had never stopped riding. However, he had never gone on to Olympic fame or world domination. Instead, he rode occasionally on the weekends and puttered away at a computer repair shop. Cycling had been relegated to the back burner of his life. The one rider who would probably have learned how to leave even Lance Armstrong in the dust had never stepped up to the line.

We all have a talent like Andrei's. Not necessarily for racing bikes, but for something else. A talent for motivating others. A talent for calming them during stressful times. A talent for expressing love through cooking, or a talent for bringing old classic cars to life.

Many of us don't even know what that talent is. Some of us do, but we don't know how to use it. Others have an inkling what it is, but the daily obligations of life seem to keep getting in the way.

Whatever the constraints are, we must make figuring out how to get past them our mission in life. Not because we owe it to ourselves. Because we owe it to others. We owe it to everyone who wishes they could do what we can, but can't.

Andrei was my best friend, but I will never forgive him for treating with such nonchalance a talent I wished to god I had, but knew I never would.

Just like there are people who will never forgive Andrei for not making the most of his talent, there are others who will never forgive me for not making the most of mine. I am not always clear on what that talent is, but I owe it to the people who love me to find it, to polish it until it shines, and to bring it to the world.

And so do you. Do it like your life depends on it, because it does.

The man at the fence

I never saw him until I moved into that place on 13th Avenue Southwest, and then I began seeing him regularly.

He would appear in the dim light before dawn or after dusk. Unsure if my momentary glimpses of him were just my eyes playing tricks on me, I would quickly look away and then glance back at him, but by that time he had noticed me noticing him and he was gone.

He usually wore a crumpled old fishing hat and a long-sleeve T-shirt with horizontal stripes. Because his hat was pulled down low over his eyes, I never saw his face clearly, just enough to know he looked a little older and his nose was a little beaky. Think Freddy Krueger from the Nightmare on Elm Street movies, but not as threatening. His spookiness did not come from him, it came from me not knowing why he was there.

I never saw what kind of pants he wore, because when I spotted him he was almost always on the other side of the fence looking in. I could tell he wasn't particularly tall, because the fence came up to the middle of his chest, while it was barely waist-high on me.

Only once did I see him inside the yard. It was almost dark out, and I had come outside on a lark, stepping off the front deck to go around to the basement door on the side of the house. He was crouched down next to a fern that grew in shade thrown off by the deck during the day. I think he was as surprised to see me as I was to see him. He disappeared instantly, gone before I could even finish turning my head to look at him.

Four years later I moved away and have not seen him since. Perhaps he was not watching me. Perhaps he was watching the house. I wonder if he appears to the people who live there now.

Learning to speak Big Kid

When I was 5 years old my family lived in Oakland, California.

We didn't live in Oakland anymore when I was 6, so I only have a few memories of that place, some random, disjointed mental pictures. A scary German Shepherd loose on the street. A teacher pinning a strip of green construction paper onto my T-shirt so the other kids wouldn't pinch me on St. Patrick's Day. A spindly-legged mosquito eater butting its head against the back wall of the house.

A kid at school had told me mosquito eaters could inflict a more painful bite than the mosquitoes themselves, so to this day I still get nervous when they are around, even though not once in my entire life has a mosquito eater ever given me any guff.

I had a friend who lived around the corner named Leo. Leo was five and a classmate of mine in the kindergarten. He also had an older sister. I don't remember ever seeing her, but she was probably about eight, and thus much older and more worldly and experienced than Leo and I could ever hope to be.

It was from Leo's sister, via Leo, that I first learned the f-word.

One day as Leo and I were outside running around playing the games 5 year old boys tend to play, I heard him muttering the phrase "f*** a ditch, f*** a ditch, f*** a ditch."

I asked him what this meant, this phrase "f*** a ditch."

"It's when a man and a woman have sex in a ditch," he said while running around in a circle.

Amazed to have stumbled upon such a useful piece of information, I stopped Leo and asked him how he had learned this phrase.

"From my sister. F*** a ditch, f*** a ditch, f*** a ditch."

I was only five, and I had an inkling sex was something men and women did together, but I didn't quite understand the mechanics of it. I hadn't yet realized men and women have different parts, so I just assumed a woman's parts looked much like a man's. How they would mate up smoothly was beyond me, but I had grown used to the fact that the world was a place full of mystery.

As for the ditch part, I just took it at face value that when adults did it, they preferred to do it in a ditch.

For the next five years I figured the f-word was the abbreviated version of the full phrase "f*** a ditch." It was not a stand-alone word for sex, and it could never be divorced from its ditch origins.

As time passed, though, the idea that adults preferred to do it in a ditch grew stranger and stranger. I started noticing men and women kissing in movies and on TV, and rarely was there a ditch nearby.

Still, I never sat down to seriously think it through. As I grew older I just picked up other pieces of the puzzle, and by the time I was ten I knew very well, thank you, that men and women had different parts, and that when they had sex, it often did not take place in ditches.

I never asked myself how ditches had entered into the picture in the first place, and then one day when I was in my mid-twenties I was at Safeway doing my weekly grocery shopping. As I reached up to pull some paper towels off the shelf a random thought came to me, "Oh, Leo's sister heard it wrong," and I burst out laughing right there in the aisle.

Thirty-six years after Leo taught it to me, that phrase still rolls smoothly off my tongue, because that's how I first learned the word.

F*** a ditch, f*** a ditch, f*** a ditch.

Twigs, rocks, dust

Under my feet I can feel twigs and rocks too small for the eye to see. A discoloration on the pavement is a thin layer of dust, not a stain. In one fluid, uninterrupted motion I hop sideways onto the street, a move I've made because I want to bypass the pavement in the crosswalk coming up, pavement that is broken and choppy because it lies at an intersection of two streets on different repaving schedules.

As I begin running up the short, shallow grade west on Galer I remind myself to resist the urge to lunge, push, power. Stay low, stay light, stay gentle. Cycle through quickly. When you wonder whether to take one step or two, take three.

It feels good to be running again. The cool morning air rushes past me, and my perspective on the city changes every few seconds as I move through it. I turn a corner here, turn a corner there, run up one hill, run down another. The sky opens up as I pass a park on the left, then closes as I run between two rows of tall buildings, then opens up again as I pass another park and run downhill towards the bay.

For the past three months I've let my running slide completely. I used to love popping my bare feet up on an ottoman in the evenings while I watched TV, flexing my toes and arches during the commercials and watching the muscles spring to life, muscles I didn't even know existed. Now my feet are just weak, passive slabs I shove into shoes each morning when I dress for work. It will take another month for the muscles to reappear.

Sometimes people think I'm kidding when I tell them I run like this, but then when the disbelief subsides they ask me three questions. The second question is usually about calluses. I tell them that I don't get calluses partly because the road is one huge emery board, but mainly because running barefoot is about learning how to run so gently walking seems violent in comparison, learning how to be physically and mentally intimate with your surroundings, reminding yourself that the barriers that limit you in life have often been erected by you, that they are there not because they are, but because you think they are.

Truck stop

I pull into a no-name truck stop north of Sacramento. I step out of the car, flick the door shut, and pause to soak up the sun's warm rays.

I know from experience the locals see the bright sun as a harbinger of the oppressive heat that will begin stifling the Valley in a few weeks, but I don't see it that way right now, because I've been in the car since northern Oregon and up there the air was cold and wet.

A few miles back was a Starbucks, but I stopped here because leaving one place to go to another is one of life's simple pleasures, and few things kill the buzz faster than the sameness of a chain.

I push through the glass door and enter the store, a bell on a string jangling against the glass as my eyes adjust to the indoor lighting. I nod at the clerk and head over to a large bank of candy bars to the left, doing a quick systems check to determine what snack will best meet my body's needs at the moment. The relative cravings for sugar, salt, flour, and fat will determine whether I buy chips, a candy bar, a hot dog, or a tuna sandwich.

I decide to go for a candy bar, but the large selection overwhelms me. Too much choice. Spotting the familiar brown and orange of a Reese's Peanut Butter Cups, I instinctively grab two and head for the refrigerated beverage case.

I pull out a chilled Starbucks "gas station mocha," partly because I like the taste, but mainly because I enjoy the friction the cap's rubberized threads make against the smooth glass, plus of course the metallic pop the cap makes when I open the bottle for the first time.

I turn from the case and head towards the register as the refrigerator door slams shut behind me. The clerk smiles at me. I pull out my wallet and briefly wonder owner or employee? It's an idle thought, as the next word out of my mouth will be "Hey" regardless.

Drunk barber

A couple weeks ago I went in for a haircut.

The barber, not my usual one, smelled like he had just recently emerged from a pool of that aftershave favored by elderly terminal alcoholics, the kind of aftershave their own dads wore, whether their own dads were alcoholics or not, the kind they must think obscures, not highlights, the reek of old drunk.

As I took a seat in the chair I thought to myself, "It'll be okay, this place hasn't steered you wrong yet, go with it, have faith and the universe will provide."

Mr. Night Train cut my hair with an insouciance I had never before encountered in a barber. He had chosen to keep my back to the mirror the entire time, so at no point could I see what he was doing. I dug deep into my pool of faith and tried not to imagine the hack job he might be doing up there.

As he cut he told me his life story. He had been a drug dealer years ago, and one of his best customers was an addict weaning his wife off heroin by getting her hooked on crack. My barber ended up stealing away with his customer's wife, marrying her, having a child with her, and then divorcing her.

He told me this story while gesticulating wildly with sharp objects in his hands. I wasn't sure whether to follow my own internal train of thought wondering about this woman and did she have second thoughts about the various choices she had made in life, or whether to key in on the tenderness and pride I could hear in this guy's voice when he talked about his daughter.

Later, when he asked me if I wanted him to shave my neck with a straight razor, I said no thanks.

But it was one of the best haircuts I've ever had.

Take a teacher to lunch

Do yourself a favor...

Look up an old teacher, someone you've thought about for years, but have lost touch with.

Google them, and try LinkedIn and Facebook. But you might have to dig around a bit to find them. You might have to go to an online phone book, or even a print version (yes, some towns still have those). Or even call the school and track them down that way. Even if they're retired now, the school will probably be able to help you find them.

Call them up, tell them a specific memory you have of them, and thank them for helping you become a better person.

And if you're in the same town, take them out to lunch.

Teachers run into old students all the time on the street. The now-grown students ask, "Hey, remember me," but the teacher can't, because the old students are now middle-aged, bald, and fifty pounds heavier.

But believe it or not, even the best teachers go years, sometimes a decade, without an old student calling them out of the blue and saying thanks, you meant a lot to me, I still think about you often after all these years.

People love to know they've changed the world around them. Especially teachers. There's a reason they do what they do.

Imagine being in their shoes, you have to spend all day surrounded by kids who act like they don't care. Then out of the blue, an old student you haven't seen in 20 years calls you and says, "Thank you so much, I've been trying to live your lessons every day for the past 20 years."

After you get a phone call like that, the next time you have to go stand up in front of a bunch of bored-looking kids, you're going to remember exactly why you do what you do.

That's a great gift to give someone. And you have it within your power to give that gift.

Besides, when you honor another person, you honor yourself.

By the way, this article was inspired by Craig Wight, who is retired now but taught shop at Mt. Whitney High, and whom I knew in 1984-85, when I was 14-15 years old. 25 years later, it was an honor to see him again and thank him for being a guide in my life every year since then.

A parting gift from my grandpa

My Grandpa Hofer passed away in 1999, when I was 29 years old. He died of pancreatic cancer. At the time of his diagnosis the doctor said he had 3 months to live. The doctor was about right.

My grandpa was a retired music teacher. I never met any of his students, so sometimes I wonder if he put onto them at least a tiny portion of the stamp he put onto me. I imagine so. After all, no matter what he was teaching, he taught by example. People remember when you teach by example, because teaching by example is so rare.

When the doctor's diagnosis came there was little debating whether to fight the cancer or not. My grandpa figured his time had come, and every moment he spent trying to prolong his life would be a moment he did not spend preparing the world for his exit.

Knowing his wife would need care he would not be around to provide, he sold the home he had built with his own two hands and moved himself and my grandma into a retirement center near my parents. My grandma still lives at that retirement center today.

My grandpa had lived most of his life within a 100-mile radius of a small farming town in central California, and he began guiding my dad on drives through the communities where he had grown up. As my dad drove along dusty, dilapidated country roads my grandpa pointed out key sites important to his life's stories. Sometimes he would ask my dad to pull over by the side of the road so they could get out and walk around and my grandpa could point out an old building or a tree that was playing a starring role in one of his stories.

Towards the end of one of these drives, my grandpa told my dad, "When I am gone, I want you to take Matt and Mark (my younger brother) on this exact same route, and I want you to tell them these exact same stories. Word for word. I want them to know where they came from." Now when I see an old barn that looks like it's about to collapse, I don't see a useless barn, I see someone's story.

About two months after the diagnosis, the cancer was ravaging his body and he was quickly growing weak. One day he picked up the phone and asked my dad to take him on an important errand. He needed to go to the funeral home to make arrangements. My dad took my grandpa to the funeral home where he picked out and paid for two adjacent plots, chose what kind of service he wanted, and picked out his own coffin. He wanted to make sure the details were taken care of early, so his family would not have to worry about them in the difficult time that was to come.

In those days I was living almost 1,000 miles to the north in Seattle, busy with a life doing work I loved, hiking in the mountains, and settling into the home I had bought earlier that year. I knew what was happening in California, though, and I kept close tabs on the situation. As the long Thanksgiving weekend approached it was clear my grandpa would not last much longer. My parents called to tell me it was time to come say goodbye. I hopped in my car and drove 16 hours overnight, arriving at my grandpa's side early on Thanksgiving morning.

In his last week my grandpa had moments when he was lucid, but he also had moments when he was not, and the moments of not were quickly becoming the majority. The family didn't have much of a Thanksgiving feast that year. No one was in the mood. Everyone was drained. We just stuck close to each other and waited together, spending most of our time at the retirement center where my grandpa was passing his last few days.

I had to be back at work in Seattle Monday morning. The night before I headed back, my mom told me it was time to say goodbye to my grandpa. I had never done anything like that before, saying goodbye to a loved one who expected me to openly acknowledge that we would never speak to each other again, at least not in this life.

There would be no empty declarations of hope for recovery. This was going to be it.

I sat in one of the side rooms down the hallway, steeling myself, trying to muster the courage to look my grandpa in the face and say my final words to him. When he was lucid enough to know who was in the room with him, my mom came down the hall to get me. "It's time," she said. I stood up and walked down the hall with her, trembling from the stress. At one point I stopped suddenly, and my mom, knowing why, turned towards me and steadied me as my knees buckled and I started sobbing. I pulled myself together again, took a deep breath, and walked the remaining few steps into the room where my grandpa lay in bed.

I knelt down next to the bed, took my grandpa's hand, dug down as deep as I could, and told him the things I knew I would never have another chance to say. I told him I loved him very much. I thanked him for the love he had shown me and the guidance he had given me over the years.

Tears streamed down my cheeks and my voice cracked with every word, but I kept on. I told him it was okay to go now, don't worry, Grandma was safe and we would take good care of her and we would make sure she never felt alone. I told him to say hello to Heather, my cousin who had passed away some years before.

My grandpa's eyes were closed and he couldn't speak, but I knew he was listening because his hand was squeezing mine, giving me the courage to say what I needed to say. I finished speaking, I squeezed his hand one last time, I kissed him on the forehead, and I stood up. I turned and hurried out of the room, unable to look anyone in the eye as I brushed past. I ran down the hall and burst out the front door to take a deep breath of the fresh night air.

A few days later I was back in Seattle when the phone rang. It was my mom. My grandpa had passed away. When he had taken his last breath, my dad had been sitting next to his bed and they were listening to one of his favorite pieces of classical music.

There are times in life when we want to collapse into a corner, to curl up into a fetal ball and shake and weep and dissolve into a trembling bunch of nerves. But in his parting gift to me my grandpa reminded me that every single one of us can choose instead to tap into a vast pool of inner strength, and when we tap into that pool we become bigger people. Those around us desperately want us to tap into it, because they are trying to tap into it too, and they need us to show them the way.

When you learn how to tap into that pool of strength, you must begin living a life that requires you to tap into that pool every single day. If you do anything less with your time here on this earth, you are wasting that time and you are wasting the gifts god gave you to use.

Since my grandpa passed away, I have tried to live this lesson every day of my life. There have been times when I have stumbled, but I have never stopped trying. I will live it until the day I die, because my grandpa lived it for me, and now I must return the favor.

Muslims are the new niggers

I have a neighbor who likes to call black people coons in private. He won't call them coons in public though. Instead, he will stop mid-sentence, smirk and wink, and say, "I have a word in mind, but I'm afraid to use it in public."

The social pressure on him does not keep him from thinking of black people as coons. But it does keep him from polluting the public space with his inner fears.

When an unknown assailant blows up a bomb in Oslo and opens fire on clean-cut white kids at summer camp, our emotions run high and we want to grab torches and a piece of rope and march off into the darkness to lynch the nasty people who did this to us.

Anger and fear and the desire for retribution are completely normal responses to an attack. Only someone cold and heartless would deny his fellow human beings the emotions that flow naturally after an event like that one.

But the strength of the emotions swirling inside of you does not relieve you of your responsibility to not pollute the public space with your fear and anger.

About a day after the attacks in Oslo, I was talking to a friend of mine. She is an intelligent, articulate person whose opinions I often disagree with, but always like to hear.

She commented on the Oslo attack and blamed it on "the Muslims."

I mentioned that the police hadn't arrested anyone yet, and that it was too early to know who did it. Her response was simply, "They have a lot of Muslim immigrants there, they are creating problems, it's a shame."

We like to tell ourselves our initial reaction to an event doesn't matter much. We like to tell ourselves that it's okay to let our emotions flow unfiltered past our lips, as long as we will let our cooler heads prevail when the facts begin to come in.

But how we choose to react in the moments immediately following an event does in fact affect what the world will look like afterwards. Our reaction might not affect who will go to jail for a particular attack. But it does affect what will and will not be acceptable drivers of our society's actions in the unrelated events that will follow in the weeks and months and years to come.

If we allow our neighbors to use the word "coon" in public, we signal to them and to others that it is okay to disrespect black people. Similarly, in the hours after an attack on Oslo, if we allow our neighbors to blame Muslims even though no one knows yet who is responsible, we signal to them and to others that it is okay to displace our anger and fear onto Muslims.

My neighbor calls black people coons because when he was growing up, people around him taught him it was socially acceptable to lash out at black people when he was feeling scared and confused. Today it is socially acceptable to lash out at Muslims when we are feeling scared and confused, as long as we tell ourselves we will allow our cooler heads to prevail when the facts come in. It is a childish way to react to the world, and we need to stop it.

Cold sweat

I wake up in a cold sweat. Mr. Dickson was just telling me I would not be graduating. I had signed up for a class and then forgotten about it. I had failed.

Wait a minute, why is the room dark? Where's Mr. Dickson, wasn't I just talking to him? I stagger to my feet and stumble to the bathroom.

I'm never going to be able to show my face around here again, my professors will be so disappointed in me.

Wait a minute, how old am I? I'm 41. I graduated 19 years ago, right? My parents were there. I wore a robe. They called my name. It happened, I know it did.

It must have been a dream. I can go back to sleep now, I don't have to get up for work for another couple hours.

For years after graduation I used to have this same dream. Then it went away. Now it's back. Why is it back, why?

Go talk to your audience

Remember the old-style modems, the ones where your computer dialed out on a phone line, and the other computer answered the call, and you could hear the two modems beeping at each other, trying to agree on a common frequency they could talk to each other on?

That's the "modem handshake."

When you start talking to another person, the two of you start with a modem handshake.

All human interactions require a modem handshake, no matter how small or large the interaction. Ordering coffee at Starbucks. Going to a job interview. Speaking to the entire country. They all start out with the modem handshake.

Sometimes, before you even open your mouth, the hair on the back of your neck stands up, and you can see in the other person's eyes that the interaction isn't going to go well. Your gut tells you the other party already has a gun pointed at your head, even before you've started to speak.

These people already made up their minds. Whatever you have to say, they're not listening. They don't even hear the words coming out of your mouth. Don't waste your time. They are not your audience.

Your audience is the people who know talking to you will require a modem handshake first, and they are willing to take a few minutes to do it.

These are the people you should be spending your time with.

Go talk to your audience.

I love running barefoot

I recently started running barefoot.

Up until a few months ago, I never liked running. In fact, for years, when people asked me if I ran, I would answer, "Only when chased."

Instead, to get my exercise, I'd head for the nearest hill. By hiking up nice steep hills, I could work myself into a frothy delirium and never risk the bodily wear and tear of running.

But these days I'm living in a place that's flat as a board. Freakishly flat, for miles and miles. So to get my exercise, I started running.

Unfortunately, running hurt like crazy. After a while the shin splints faded away, but there was this one small area of my inner calf that hurt no matter what I did.

I tried different kinds of shoes, different orthotics and arch supports, even an insert that you had to bake in the oven before you used it the first time.

But the same pain kept coming back. I gave up running, figuring I'd just have to make do with walking really fast.

Then I heard about running barefoot, and I decided to give it a try. After all, what did I have to lose?

Oh. My. God. I LOVE IT!!!

The muscles used, and the motions made, are completely different than in regular running. Instead of landing on your heel, rolling forward, and pushing off with your toes, you land on the front of your foot, gently touch your heel to the ground, and then lift your entire foot off the ground.

When I first started out, I wore Vibram Fivefingers. But I kept reading that when you are learning how to run barefoot, you should go completely barefoot on the hardest pavement you can find.

I thought that sounded a little extreme. Surely, keeping at least a little bit of rubber between my feet and the ground, and spending most of my time on dirt and grass, would be the best way to ease into it.

But one day, I figured I'd take off my Vibrams and see what happened. And it was amazing.

A hard cement sidewalk is a completely unforgiving environment in which to run barefoot, so you have no choice but to do it right, and your body will give you immediate feedback if you do it wrong.

As a result, from the very first step, running barefoot on cement is amazingly smooth and gentle.

In fact, it's more gentle than running in shoes. I know, it's totally counter-intuitive. But it turns out it's so true.

Muscles I didn't even know existed are appearing in my feet now, but other than that, at the end of the day my feet feel like they did nothing all day but walk around on padded carpets.

Now, if you run in shoes, and if it's working for you, don't lie awake at night wondering if you should try running barefoot. It's like starting all over again -- new muscles, new technique, new everything. Even if you're a seasoned runner, it'll be a month before you're ready to run even one mile barefoot. If it ain't broke, don't fix it.

But if you want to run, but can't because it hurts, or if you just want to get back in touch with your inner Kalahari bushman, give it a shot. It's not just exercise. It's zen.

Egg, cheese, toast

I lift the egg from the stove and slide it onto cheese melted over wheat toast. A favorite breakfast of mine. Break the egg's yolk and it becomes a lazy man's Eggs Benedict.

Where is the Canadian bacon, you might ask, suggesting that perhaps you do not understand what I mean when I call it the "lazy man's Eggs Benedict."

The kitchen is small but it serves its purpose just fine. A window looks out over Elliott Bay, Alki to the south and Bainbridge to the west. Ferries crisscross the bay and on Sundays cargo ships from Asia dock at terminals I can't see because a tree is in the way.

A storm moves north over Alki towards me. Actually, Seattle rarely has storms, it just has "permawet." I know before I leave the apartment the umbrella will come in handy this morning.

It's 6:05 but I delay my departure a moment while I finish reading a magazine article. The article is not particularly interesting, but I'm almost done and I want to finish it. At 6:06 I drop the magazine on the table, put the dishes in the sink, and walk towards the door, relaxed in the knowledge that as long as I leave by 6:09 I'll be okay.

You don't get to blame society

The other day I was listening to the radio. They were talking about the lack of civility in society, and how people were feeling more disconnected and less satisfied. They were talking about Americans' focus on GDP (Gross Domestic Product), and the need for an alternative measure, like Bhutan's Gross National Happiness.

They were talking about how people are rude to each other, how people are alienated from each other, etc.

I'm sorry, but when you want to complain about human relations in your society, you don't get to blame society. You don't get to blame anyone but yourself, and you don't get to propose solutions that are anything except, "I will treat my fellow man better."

When you walk up to the counter at Wendy's, you have to treat that clerk with respect. You have to look him in the eye, and you have to say please, and you have to say thank you. You have to treat that clerk just like you would want to be treated if you were the one standing behind that counter.

You don't get to treat that clerk like a piece of cardboard standing between you and your hamburger. You don't get to say, "The clerk at Best Buy was rude to me a half hour ago, so since everyone else is lowering the standards, I am going to lower them too."

And yes, when you start treating people well, lots of people are still going to treat you badly. You're going to have plenty of times when you feel tired and say to yourself, "Why do I have to treat this Wendy's clerk with respect, no one treats me with respect, I'll get lazy and be rude to this Wendy's clerk just this one time."

Groups don't change when people stand around and point fingers at each other and say, "I'll change when he does." Groups change when people take individual actions.

But you're not treating people with respect for something in return. You're doing this for yourself. It will remind you that you have power over yourself, and that there is joy in exercising it.

Like Gandhi said, "You must be the change you want to see in the world."

My cousin's name is Jihad

Before I lived in Turkey, I thought the word "jihad" was a word of hate and violence. I associated that word with crazed lunatics, suicide bombers blowing themselves up in public squares, and people flying airplanes into tall buildings.

But then I went to Turkey, and I started meeting people named Jihad!

I remember this one day in particular, when I met my first Jihad. He was my wife's cousin (actually, his name was "Cihat," the Turkish spelling of "Jihad").

My wife and I went to this beautiful tea garden, one of our favorite tea gardens in all of Istanbul.

We met up with my wife's cousin, his wife, and their kids. And this guy, this cousin, his name was Cihat!

Cihat carried himself with the pious, thoughtful nature of a deeply religious man. His wife had a conservative headscarf tightly wound around her head and neck, and she wore the plain, long, beige-colored overcoat even my new eyes recognized as the mark of a socially and religiously conservative woman.

Their kids, a young boy and a young girl, carried themselves in the poised, well-mannered way you often see in kids who are growing up in a religious household.

But this guy with the radical, violent name, he was just a big teddy bear. You could see it in his eyes, in his face, in the way he looked at his wife and kids. You could even hear it in the way he talked to me, a godless, heathen foreigner he had just met.

Cihat was one the gentlest souls I had ever met.

That afternoon, I was feeling a little confused, wondering, my god, how can this gentle teddy bear of a man have a crazy, violent, hateful name like Cihat? What on earth were his parents thinking? Did they even know what that word meant?

Turns out I was the one who didn't know what that word meant. Because in the months that followed, I met tons of Cihats in Turkey. Cihat is actually a pretty common guy's name in Turkey. It's like being named Paul, or Mark, or Bob. And when someone comes up to you and says, "Hi, my name is Bob," you don't panic and run for the hills, do you?

So I figured, the parents must know something I don't. After all, it doesn't matter where in the world you are, parents love their children. No parent in the world is going to give his kid a hateful, violent name.

I decided to look into what this word meant, jihad. And here's what I found...

The word "jihad" has multiple meanings. And yes, "violent war against an external infidel" is one of them. But that is not the primary meaning of the word. It is not the mainstream, popular meaning of the word.

The word jihad more often means "struggle to cleanse your own heart of sin." It means to purge your heart of sin, to live God's word in your own heart. Never mind the other people, just purify your own soul.

I didn't go to some obscure, Middle East-loving, crazy peacenik source to find this definition. I just went to Wikipedia. I went to Wikipedia and typed in "jihad." And then just to verify what I learned, I went to a couple other mainstream American websites like Yahoo, and Ask.com.

This other meaning, "purging your own heart of sin," is a mainstream, widely-accepted meaning. In fact, it is the majority meaning of this word. Most of the people who use this word mean "purge the infidel within your own heart."

Now, I'm not saying that suicide bombers are peace-loving, gentle souls. I am saying that for every crazed lunatic, there are thousands of gentle, loving souls who say jihad is about purifying your own heart. They are saying never mind the non-believers, our hands are full just living God's words in our own hearts.

This phenomenon is common to pretty much every religion around the world. Take Christianity, for example. For every Christian who thinks Christianity is about grabbing a sword and slaying the heathens in the name of the Lord, there are thousands who say Christianity is about saying, "Never mind the heathens, my job is to purify my own heart."

It means our conventional-wisdom, popular understanding of the word "jihad" is ridiculously myopic.

And if we're myopic about that, what else are we myopic about?

When we meet someone else, someone from another religion, or another country, or another job or social class, it is our duty to that person to remind ourselves that our understanding of that person is probably incorrect.

And it is our duty to humanity to try to overcome that incorrectness.

After all, when we allow an incorrect understanding to drive our actions, those actions will be misguided. And even if we do reach our goal, we will probably find out, too late, that we have chosen the wrong one.

More than just groceries

I went to Walmart to pick up some groceries today. When I had everything I needed, I went to the checkout lane, and the cashier started ringing up my stuff.

I was off in my own little world, caught up in my own little self-pity party. It had been kind of a rough week for me. I wasn't feeling too good about being me at that particular moment.

The cashier started making small talk. She asked if I was having a good Father's Day. I replied that I was having an excellent Father's Day, thank you (a little white lie, since actually I was busy thinking about how hard my life was).

She asked me if I was a father, and I smiled and said, "No, but I have one." She smiled back and replied, "I think we all do." I said, "Yes, I guess it tends to work that way."

There was a moment of silence, while she continued ringing up my groceries.

Then I asked her, "How about you, do you have any children?"

And she said, "Well, yes, we had three, but they are in Heaven now."

This woman was about 25 years old, and she had already buried three children.

No matter how much you might be thinking your current situation sucks, the person standing next to you is probably going through a tough time of their own, too.

And in fact, theirs might be worse than yours.

The first thing you should know

The first thing you should know about anywhere in the world is that the people there relate to their world a whole lot more like the way you relate to yours, rather than the way you think they relate to theirs, or the way you relate to theirs, or the way you think they relate to yours.

You might need to travel the world to actually see that in action.

But the funny thing about travel is, the more you do it, the more you realize you don't really need it to understand other people.

Looking, finding, ignoring

I went looking for something but could never find it. I did find something else, but I ignored it so I could keep looking for the thing I could never find.

The ripples are why the cake tastes so good

My Grandpa Krause has been building and fixing things longer than I've been alive. He's a farmer by trade, and for decades he used a tractor that was new back in the days of the Korean War. That tractor is still around, and it runs just fine. Half the parts on that thing were made by him, simply because it's hard to find ready-made parts for a machine that old.

He retired from farming a few years back, and now he teaches 8- to 10-year old kids how to build birdhouses, bookcases, and storage chests. The kids conceive and design their own projects and learn how to use the tools they need to build them. The other day, I went to the graduation ceremony for one of these classes.

Those kids worshipped him, and the parents loved him for teaching their kids a skill and, more so, for being the kind of man their kids could worship.

As soon as I showed up for the ceremony, and the kids and their parents realized I was "Mr. Krause's grandson," they worshipped and loved me, too. And I hadn't even done anything except walk into the room.

For a few hours, I got to feel like a rock star, and I didn't even know how to play the guitar. The gift my grandpa had given those kids was rippling out and affecting me, too.

When you give a gift to someone, the beneficiary isn't just the recipient. It's everyone the recipient will come across in the future.

You owe it to your country

The sad thing about this photo isn't the unemployed people. It's not even the factory or the town going downhill.

The sad thing about this photo is the guys who wrote the sign were basically telling the world, "We are such bad businessmen, such unimaginative people, that even if someone came up to us who could take $5 and turn it into $10, we are so busy dying that we can't talk to that person."

That's an incredible, and embarrassing, lack of faith in yourself.

For 20 years, we, the United States, have been playing consumer to the world. Now we, and much of the world, are paying the price. What got us here won't get us where we want to go next, and it will take us a while to figure out what that next is going to look like. In the meantime, we get to have a recession.

The spirit that caused those people to write that sign, I see a lot of that spirit going around these days. It's the spirit of, "We are so busy dying we don't have time to live."

Find that spirit within yourself, and root it out like there's no tomorrow. You owe it to yourself, and you owe it to your country.

Starbucks

The neighborhood Starbucks serves as my office these days. It's got an internet connection, a place to sit for a couple hours, and it's there when I need it, out of mind when I don't.

I walk in and pull a bottled Mocha Frappuccino out of the refrigerator case. I call these "the gas station mochas," because they sell the same thing at gas station convenience stores. I started buying them because they're the cheapest thing in the store, $1.85 and you can hog a table for hours without feeling guilty. I suppose I could upgrade to a more expensive, custom-made drink now, but it's become habit.

Plus, I enjoy pulling the perforated plastic seal off the top, trying to get it in one smooth pull so I don't have a bunch of tiny plastic scraps sitting around. It's a little game I like to play each morning.

My favorite table is available, a small round table pushed up against one of the walls. It's big enough for one, too small for two. I take a seat, enjoying the fact that at a regular coffee joint you have anonymity when you want it, familiar faces when you don't.

As I sit there waiting for my computer to boot up, I stare out the window, dreaming, eyes fixated on something but seeing nothing. For some reason, I get lost in the memory of my first car, a beige Volkswagen, bought for $800 from an elderly couple in Mabton, a small town in Washington State.

A year or two after I got that Volkswagen, I moved onto something else, and I gave the car to my dad. He ran it until the engine blew up along a two-lane highway in Eastern Washington. He got a friend to pick him up and then he put an ad in the paper: "Abandoned car on Highway 24, the car is free if you'll take it away."

He tells me that a couple years later, he saw that same car, revived and tooling around the backroads again. Now, over twenty years later, I imagine that if I drove around that part of the state long enough, I'd still see it.

My computer beeps to tell me it finished booting up, so I reluctantly reenter the present and begin my day.

If you liked *Soapbox*:

- Post a review on the book's Amazon page.
- Check out Matt's book *A Tight Wide-open Space*, available in paperback, on Kindle, and as a podcast series on iTunes.
- Read Matt's weekly column "Dispatches from Somewhere," syndicated in newspapers around the world or on his website at www.mattkrause.com.

If you would like to host a virtual book party, gather some friends and Matt will join you via Skype (see www.mattkrause.com for details).

And of course, you can spread the love and pass this book along to a friend!

Soapbox is available in paperback, on Kindle, and as a podcast series on iTunes.

Pass it on…

If you enjoyed this book, someone else will too. Write down a few names that come to mind, and then pass it on. Remember to cross your name off the list before you do.

_____

_____

_____

_____

_____

_____

_____

Please return this book to:
_____

Made in the USA
Charleston, SC
09 July 2012